W9-ATY-569

SNAKES/ LAS SERPIENTES

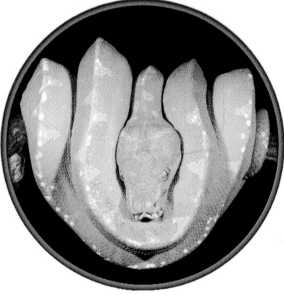

by JoAnn Early Macken

Reading consultant: Susan Nations, M.Ed., author/literacy coach/consultant

WEEKLY WR READER®
EARLY LEARNING LIBRARY

Please visit our web site at: www.garethstevens.com
For a free color catalog describing our list of high-quality books,
call 1-800-542-2595 (USA) or 1-800-387-3178 (Canada).

Library of Congress Cataloging-in-Publication Data available upon request from publisher.
Fax (414) 336-0157 for the attention of the Publishing Records Department.

ISBN-10: 0-8368-4385-1 (lib. bdg.)
ISBN-13: 978-0-8368-4385-9 (lib. bdg.)
ISBN-10: 0-8368-4390-8 (softcover)
ISBN-13: 978-0-8368-4390-3 (softcover)

This edition first published in 2004 by
Weekly Reader® Books
An imprint of Gareth Stevens Publishing
1 Reader's Digest Road
Pleasantville, NY 10570-7000 USA

Copyright © 2002 by Weekly Reader® Early Learning Library

Art direction: Tammy West
Production: Susan Ashley
Photo research: Diane Laska-Swanke
Graphic design: Katherine A. Goedheer
Translation: Colleen Coffey and Consuelo Carrillo

Photo credits: Cover, title, pp. 17, 21 © James P. Rowan; p. 5 © William Muñoz; p. 7 © Richard
Thom/Visuals Unlimited; p. 9 © Jim Merli/Visuals Unlimited; p. 11 © Joel Arrington/Visuals
Unlimited; p. 13 © Bayard Brattstrom/Visuals Unlimited; p. 15 © Gilbert Twiest/Visuals Unlimited;
p. 19 © Bill Draker/KAC Productions

Printed in the United States of America

2 3 4 5 6 7 8 9 10 09 08 07

Note to Educators and Parents

Reading is such an exciting adventure for young children! They are beginning to integrate their oral language skills with written language. To encourage children along the path to early literacy, books must be colorful, engaging, and interesting; they should invite the young reader to explore both the print and the pictures.

Animals I See at the Zoo is a new series designed to help children read about twelve fascinating animals. In each book, young readers will learn interesting facts about the featured animal.

Each book is specially designed to support the young reader in the reading process. The familiar topics are appealing to young children and invite them to read — and re-read — again and again. The full-color photographs and enhanced text further support the student during the reading process.

In addition to serving as wonderful picture books in schools, libraries, homes, and other places where children learn to love reading, these books are specifically intended to be read within an instructional guided reading group. This small group setting allows beginning readers to work with a fluent adult model as they make meaning from the text. After children develop fluency with the text and content, the book can be read independently. Children and adults alike will find these books supportive, engaging, and fun!

Una nota a los educadores y a los padres

¡La lectura es una emocionante aventura para los niños! En esta etapa están comenzando a integrar su manejo del lenguaje oral con el lenguaje escrito. Para fomentar la lectura desde una temprana edad, los libros deben ser vistosos, atractivos e interesantes; deben invitar al joven lector a explorar tanto el texto como las ilustraciones.

Animales que veo en el zoológico es una nueva serie pensada para ayudar a los niños a conocer cuatro animales fascinantes. En cada libro, los jóvenes lectores conocerán datos interesantes sobre ellos.

Cada libro ha sido especialmente diseñado para facilitar el proceso de lectura. La familiaridad con los temas tratados atrae la atención de los niños y los invita a leer — y releer — una y otra vez. Las fotografías a todo color y el tipo de letra facilitan aún más al estudiante el proceso de lectura.

Además de servir como fantásticos libros ilustrados en la escuela, la biblioteca, el hogar y otros lugares donde los niños aprenden a amar la lectura, estos libros han sido concebidos específicamente para ser leídos en grupos de instrucción guiada. Este contexto de grupos pequeños permite que los niños que se inician en la lectura trabajen con un adulto cuya fluidez les sirve de modelo para comprender el texto. Una vez que se han familiarizado con el texto y el contenido, los niños pueden leer los libros por su cuenta. ¡Tanto niños como adultos encontrarán que estos libros son útiles, entretenidos y divertidos!

— Susan Nations, M.Ed., author, literacy coach,
and consultant in literacy development

I like to go to the zoo.
I see snakes at the zoo.

Me gusta ir al zoológico.
En el zoológico veo
serpientes.

Some snakes climb trees.
Green snakes can hide in
the leaves.

- - - - - - - -

Algunas serpientes
trepan por los árboles.
Las serpientes verdes se
pueden esconder entre
las hojas.

Some snakes live under the ground. They dig nests under the ground.

— — — — — — — —

Algunas serpientes viven bajo el suelo. Cavan nidos bajo el suelo.

Some snakes swim in water. They move from side to side as they swim.

— — — — — — —

Algunas serpientes nadan en el agua. Se mueven de un lado a otro cuando nadan.

Some snakes live in the **desert**. They leave **trails** as they **glide** in the sand.

- - - - - - - -

Algunas serpientes viven en el **desierto**. Dejan un **rastro** cuando **se deslizan** en la arena.

trails/
rastros

Some snakes have marks
to help them hide. Can you
see the snake in this picture?

- - - - - - -

Algunas serpientes tienen
marcas en la piel que las
ayudan a esconderse.
¿Puedes ver la serpiente
de esta foto?

Snakes smell with their tongues. They find food with their tongues.

— — — — — — —

Las serpientes huelen con la lengua. Encuentran la comida con la lengua.

Snakes do not hear well. They know that **danger** is near when they feel the ground shake.

- - - - - - - -

Las serpientes no oyen bien. Saben que hay un **peligro** cerca cuando sienten que el suelo se mueve.

I like to see snakes
at the zoo. Do you?

— — — — — — —

Me gusta ver las
serpientes en el
zoológico. ¿Y a ti?

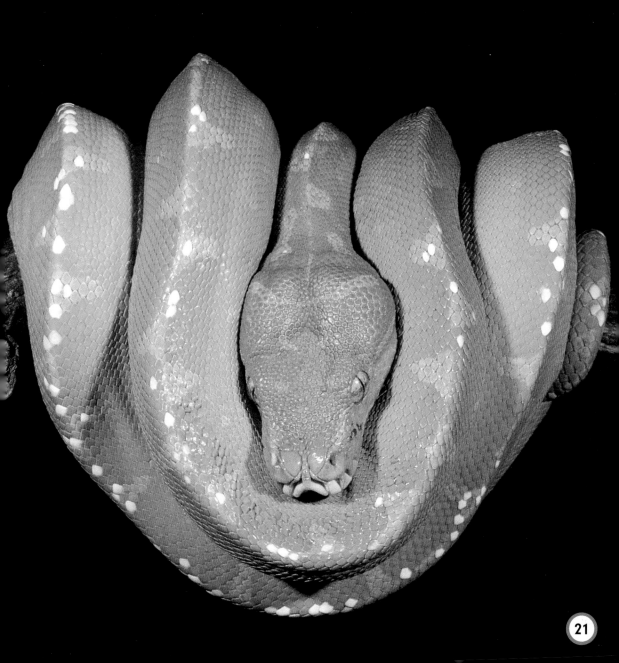

Glossary/Glosario

danger — something that may cause harm

peligro — algo que puede hacer daño

desert — dry land with few plants

desierto — terreno seco con pocas plantas

glide — to move smoothly and easily

deslizarse — moverse suavemente y con facilidad

trails — marks left by a moving body

rastros — marcas que deja un cuerpo en movimiento

For More Information/Más información

Books/Libros

Ling, Mary, and Mary Atkinson. *The Snake Book.*
New York: Dorling Kindersley, 2000.

Macken, JoAnn Early. *Rain Forest Animals. Animal Worlds*
(series). Milwaukee: Gareth Stevens, 2002.

Patent, Dorothy Hinshaw. *Slinky Scaly Slithery Snakes.*
New York: Walker and Co., 2000.

Simon, Seymour. *Snakes.* New York: HarperCollins, 1992.

Web Sites/Páginas Web

Lincoln Park Zoo

zoo.interaccess.com/tour/factsheets/herps/ball_python.html
For a ball python photo and facts
zoo.interaccess.com/tour/factsheets/herps/g_t_python.html
For a green tree python photo and facts

Woodland Park Zoo

www.zoo.org/educate/fact_sheets/day/boa_c.htm
For a boa constrictor photo, map, and facts

Index/Índice

About the Author/Información sobre la autora

JoAnn Early Macken is the author of two rhyming picture books, Sing-Along Song and Cats on Judy, and four other series of nonfiction books for beginning readers. Her poems have appeared in several children's magazines. A graduate of the M.F.A. in Writing for Children and Young Adults program at Vermont College, she lives in Wisconsin with her husband and their two sons. Visit her Web site at www.joannmacken.com.

JoAnn Early Macken es autora de dos libros infantiles ilustrados en verso, Sing-Along Song y Cats on Judy, y también de cuatro series de libros de corte realista dirigidos a los lectores principiantes. Sus poemas han sido publicados en varias revistas para niños. Graduada del M.F.A. en Redacción para niños y adultos jóvenes del Vermont College, vive en Wisconsin con su esposo y sus dos hijos. Visita su página Web. www.joannmacken.com.